artworld

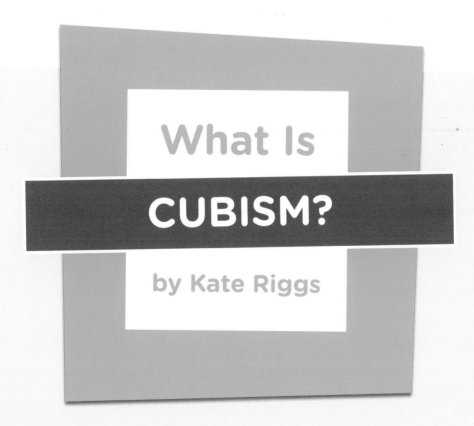

What Is

CUBISM?

by Kate Riggs

CREATIVE EDUCATION • CREATIVE PAPERBACKS

Published by Creative Education and Creative Paperbacks
P.O. Box 227, Mankato, Minnesota 56002
Creative Education and Creative Paperbacks are
imprints of The Creative Company
www.thecreativecompany.us

Design and production by Chelsey Luther
Art direction by Rita Marshall
Printed in the United States of America

Photographs by Alamy (Heritage Image Partnership Ltd), Art Resource
(Georges Braque/2015 Artists Rights Society [ARS], New York/ADAGP,
Paris), The Bridgeman Art Library (Musee National d'Art Moderne, Centre
Pompidou, Paris, France/Peter Willi/Bridgeman Images) Corbis (Marcel
Duchamp/Philadelphia Museum of Art, Juan Gris/Burstein Collection,
Juan Gris/Geoffrey Clements, Jean Metzinger/Burstein Collection, Jean
Metzinger/Francis G. Mayer, Pablo Picasso/The Gallery Collection, Pablo
Picasso/Francis G. Mayer, Lyubov Popova/Catherine Leblanc/Godong,
Jacques Villon/Philadelphia Museum of Art, Max Weber/Francis G. Mayer)

Library of Congress Cataloging-in-Publication Data
Riggs, Kate.
What is cubism? / Kate Riggs.
p. cm. — (Art world)
Summary: With prompting questions and historical background, an
early reader comes face to face with famous works of Cubist art and is
encouraged to identify shapes and consider points of view.
Includes bibliographical references and index.
ISBN 978-1-60818-624-2 (hardcover)
ISBN 978-1-62832-222-4 (pbk)
ISBN 978-1-56660-690-5 (eBook)
1. Cubism—Juvenile literature. I. Title.

N6494.C8R54 2016
709.04'032—dc23   2015008495

CCSS: RI.1.1, 2, 3, 5, 6, 7; RI.2.1, 2, 3, 5, 6, 7; RI.3.1, 3, 5, 7; RF.1.1; RF.2.3, 4;
RF.3.3

First Edition HC
9 8 7 6 5 4 3 2 1
First Edition PBK
9 8 7 6 5 4 3 2 1

Contents

Bending Lines

What do you see in a painting? If you see a lot of shapes and colors, you may be looking at Cubism.

Russian Ballet (1916), by Max Weber

Above: *Portrait of a Philosopher* (1915), by Lyubov Popova
Right: *Portrait of Chess Players* (1911), by Marcel Duchamp

Taking Shape

A cube is a block. Cubism is all about shape and form. Cubist paintings look as if you could touch them.

Painting Friends

Two friends started Cubism in Paris, France. Pablo Picasso and Georges Braque painted people and landscapes. But people in their pictures had sharp edges. Objects were split into many pieces.

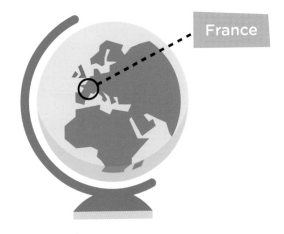

France

Factory at Horta de Ebro (1909), by Picasso

Same but Different

Braque and Picasso worked together closely.
Look at Picasso's *The Accordionist* (1911).

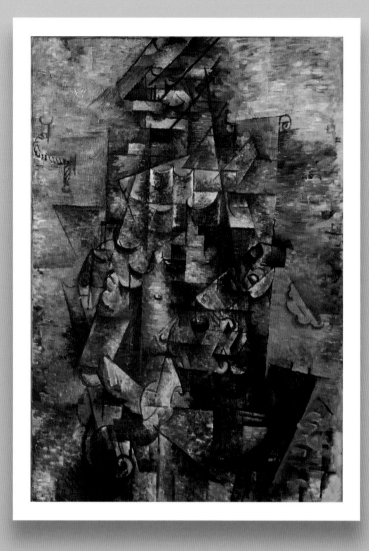

Now look at Braque's *Man with a Guitar* (1912). Both use dark colors and shadows. All the shapes group in the middle.

Left: *The Accordionist*; above: *Man with a Guitar*

All in View

It is easier to see Juan Gris's *Violin and Guitar* (1913). He used bold colors. But Gris chopped everything into shapes, too. Cubists liked using different points of view. We can see three sides of the violin instead of one.

How many upright lines can you see?

Puzzle Pieces

Cubist portraits play with point of view. Gris's *Portrait of the Artist's Mother* (1912) looks like a puzzle. The face seems stretched out. The ears are not straight across.

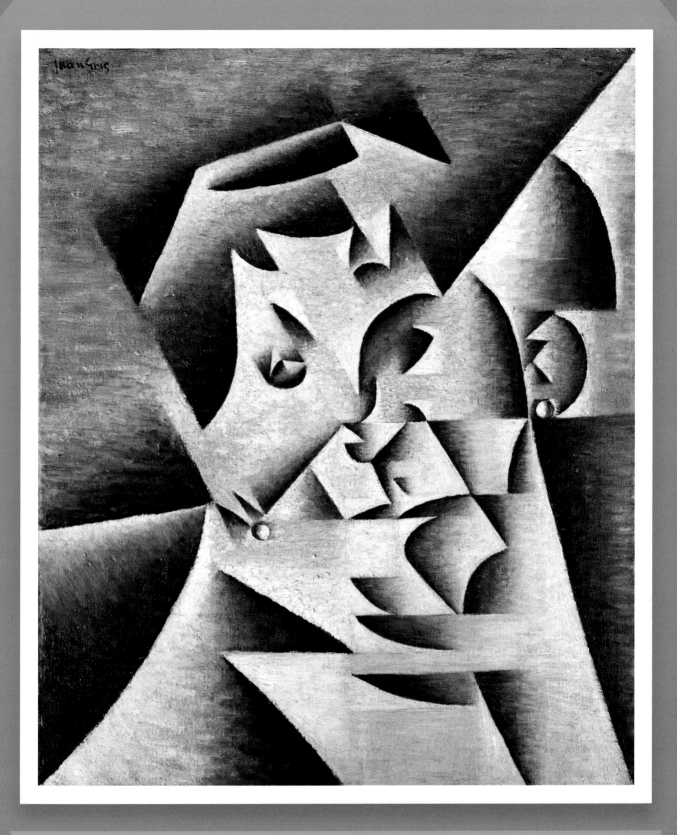

This painting is also known as *Head of a Woman*.

Stacks of Shapes

In *Young Woman (Girl)* (1912), the body looks like a stack of shapes. Jacques Villon painted this. He learned about Cubism from Picasso and Braque. He liked to build shapes and make patterns.

The pyramid shape (with sides that are triangles) is used here.

Cubism and You

What do you see in a Cubist painting? How many shapes can you find? Look for the patterns in real life, too!

Name the shapes in Metzinger's *Dancer in a Cafe* (1912).

Portrait of a Cubist

Jean Metzinger was an early Cubist. He was born in France in 1883. Jean tried to use many points of view in a single painting. Then viewers could see everything from different angles.

Left: *The Knitter* (1919); above: *Woman with a Fan* (1913)

Glossary

landscapes—pictures about the countryside

patterns—lines or shapes that are repeated

points of view—what you see based on where you are standing or at which side you are looking

portraits—paintings of people, usually showing their faces

Read More

Anholt, Laurence. *Picasso and the Girl with a Ponytail*. London: Barron's, 2007.

Winter, Jonah. *Just Behave, Pablo Picasso!* New York: Arthur A. Levine, 2012.

Websites

Art Projects for Kids
http://artprojectsforkids.org/how-to-draw-a-cubist-portrait/
Learn how to draw a Cubist portrait.

Destination: Modern Art
http://www.moma.org/interactives/destination/
Travel to the Museum of Modern Art, with the help of a friendly alien.

Index